The Whirly Bird

The Whirly Bird

by

Dimitry Varley

illustrated by

Feodor Rojankovsky

Alfred A. Knopf   •   New York

L. C. Catalog card number: 60-5507

THIS IS A BORZOI BOOK
PUBLISHED BY ALFRED A. KNOPF, INC.

MOTHER ROBIN had built her nest on a bend in a drain-pipe, snug and sheltered, right under the roof of Jenny's house. It was made of twigs and grass and looked prickly from the outside. Inside, where Mother Robin had laid and hatched her eggs, it was soft and cozy.

6319

Now four thin necks stretched from the nest, and four shrill voices chirped loudly. Mother Robin's babies were ten days old and they were always hungry and calling for more food. They were growing fast and the nest was becoming crowded as the little robins pushed and jostled one another.

Time had come to learn to fly. The four robins were excited and impatient. Father Robin had said he would teach them soon and each baby bird wanted to be the first to have a lesson. "You will be last," they teased the youngest and smallest bird.

But he was just as eager to fly as the others and he knew he was ready to learn. Besides, nobody likes to be teased. Stretching himself to his full height, he teetered to the very edge of the nest, opened his wings, and began flapping them. And then . . . he lost his balance . . . and fell.

It was a long way from the roof to the ground. He fluttered his wings wildly but he only kept falling. When at last he landed on the grass he was shaken and out of breath, but not really hurt. He was the first out of the nest, after all! He chirped loudly to tell the others, but no one answered. He chirped again, more pitifully now, but there was no mother or father to hear. He was quite alone.

Soon it began to get dark. "Is the Cat waiting to pounce on me?" he worried. Mother Robin had warned them about the Cat and he felt cold shivers of fear. "I wouldn't have a chance even to peep," he thought. And again he tried to fly. But he just tumbled out onto the path where he lay helplessly on his side, panting.

Jenny was riding her bike along the path and spied him. "A baby robin has fallen from the nest!" she shouted, and she rushed to pick him up.

The small robin struggled hard in the palm of Jenny's hand, but her fingers held him gently and firmly so that he would not get hurt trying to free himself. She lifted him toward her face. He closed his eyes, his heart thumping. "This must be the Cat," he thought. "Now I am lost . . . she will eat me." But he felt only Jenny's warm breath. "Perhaps she is not hungry now," he said to himself, "and will eat me later."

Warmed by Jenny's hand, the robin quieted down. Jenny found a cardboard box, put some soft rags and bits of dry grass on the bottom, and then, ever so gently, she placed the little bird in it. Then she picked up the box and carried it, carefully and steadily, into the house. The robin was so tired he fell asleep in a twinkling.

Morning came. It was dark in the bottom of the box when the robin woke, and he didn't know where he was. Where were the other birds? "Chirp . . . Chirp. . . ." He called his mother as loudly as he could. But she was nowhere around. He hopped toward the wall of the box and threw himself against it, trying to jump out, but each time he fell on his back. At last he remembered falling out of the nest.

Jenny heard the robin's chirping as she came down to breakfast. Quickly she got some canned dog food. He was more used to fat worms and ripe cherries, but Jenny had none and she knew baby robins can be fed canned dog food. She also knew she should not give the bird any water, because dog food has enough moisture in it. Young robins might die if they drink water.

The robin was sulking in a
corner of the box when Jenny
stooped to pick him up. He was

indignant when she grasped him firmly, opened his mouth wide with two fingers, and used a match-stick to push a little lump of dog food down deep in his throat. He nearly choked. But that food, that canned dog food, did not taste bad at all. Strange, not like anything he had ever eaten before, but not bad. Next time Jenny held food over his head, he opened his mouth wide, and another bit of food was stuffed into his open mouth.

Jenny fed him several times that morning, but in a few minutes he was calling again for more, and Jenny knew she could never feed him as often as he needed to be fed. Baby birds have small bodies and small stomachs. They can eat only a very little at a time but they have huge appetites and must be fed often. "How can I possibly feed him every ten min-utes?" Jenny worried. She would have liked to put him back into his nest but that was way out of reach.

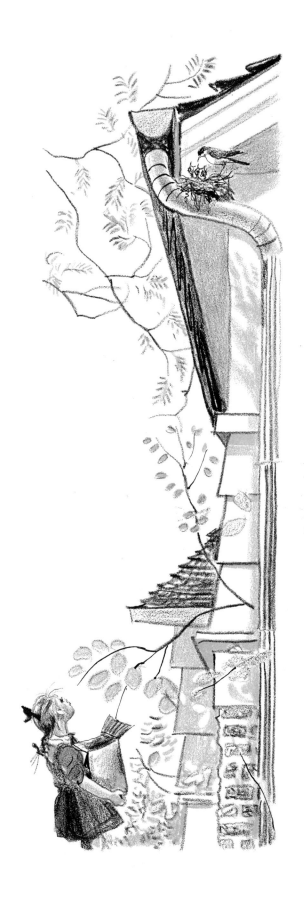

And then Jenny had an idea. She picked up the box, took it out of the house, and placed it in a clearing among the bushes. "Perhaps his parents will hear his chirping and come," she thought. She sat quietly and patiently a short distance away and waited to see what would happen. She wanted to guard the robin because she knew the Cat was lurking about.

The baby robin was glad to breathe fresh air again and to see

blue sky. But he was lonesome for his family and called to them loudly. "Chirp . . . chirp!" He was hungry again, too. Jenny could hear the thumping in the box as the robin threw himself against its walls, over and over again, until he was too exhausted to move and his chirping grew fainter.

"He is getting very tired," thought Jenny. She was ready to take him back into the house.

Suddenly, high on the branch of a maple tree, Jenny saw a grown-up robin, hopping excitedly. His mother had heard him! Mother Robin called back, "Cheep . . . cheep . . . cheep." And the baby robin answered with as loud a chirp as he could manage.

But where was her youngest robin, wondered Mother Robin. She cocked her head this way and that, her bright eyes searching the ground. She flew to a lower branch, then to a bush below. Then she dared to sail down and sit on the edge of the box from which the chirping seemed to come. Yes, there he was. What was he doing in that box? But the important thing now was food—he had to be fed.

Mother Robin flew off, and was back in no time with a juicy
brown worm hanging from her beak. She flew from one branch to
another and then to the box. She was afraid of the deep dark box
but the baby robin was pleading loudly. She dipped down into the
box, thrust the worm into his open beak, and flew out. Then his
father came bringing more food. Jenny sighed with relief. Now the
robin would not be hungry.

Well-fed and warmed by the sun, he felt content and drowsy. Jenny left for lunch. And the little robin's parents went off to feed the other babies. His eyes were half-closed in sleep when he suddenly heard a strange noise. He looked up . . . straight into the face of the Cat. The Cat was flat on his belly on a tree stump, his eyes fixed on the robin, his soft short paws bent, his tail swishing slowly in wide half circles. The little robin was struck with terror. He threw back his head, his fuzzy down stiffened, and his little claws dug into the cardboard floor of the box.

"What can I do? Is there no one to help me?" the robin cried to himself, and closed his eyes. At that very moment Jenny came running from the house, her shiny yellow braids flying. She had seen it all from the window and hoped she would not be too late. "Shoo!" she screamed.

The Cat jumped down, looked at Jenny with angry eyes, and then, disappointed and still hungry, quickly slunk away. There is no animal as strong as Jenny, thought the robin gratefully. He even let her stroke his head, though he was still so scared he sat down on his tail.

To keep him safe, Jenny placed the box on a chair on the porch. "Now it will not be easy for the Cat to reach you," she told him.

The robin's parents soon found the new spot, but much more daring was needed to feed him. The parents had to fly under the roof of the porch and into the box. Birds do not like to do that. But when they know one of their babies has to be fed, they have all the courage needed.

As darkness fell, Mother and Father Robin went away for the night. The baby robin fell asleep in a corner and Jenny moved the box carefully into the house and covered it with a cloth.

And after that, each morning before breakfast she put him back on the porch stool and all day his parents brought him bits of food. He began to grow by leaps and bounds. Jenny could almost see him grow under her very eyes. He was getting stronger, too, alert and active like his father.

And each day he tried again to get out of the box. He would jump, or rather fly, higher and higher, again and again, until one day Jenny saw he almost reached the top of the box. Although he was beginning to grow real feathers over the soft baby-bird down, he was still too young to be let out.

Jenny found an even deeper box for the robin and dropped a few small sticks in it for him to perch on. He clawed and struggled furiously as he was lowered into his new quarters and he immediately tried again to fly out. Higher and higher he went, flapping his wings as fast as he could. But freedom was still far away.

Several more days passed. The robin grew plump and strong and new bright feathers were coming in beautifully.

"He is a handsome young robin," said Jenny proudly, "healthy and strong. He is strong enough to fly almost straight up in the box."

At last Jenny decided it was time to let him go. She chose a moment when his parents were nearby. She tilted the box slightly and the robin, with a single strong effort, was out . . . FREE. He perched for a moment on the porch railing and then dropped to the lawn. His parents came over, calling to him, wanting to teach him to fly.

But he didn't need to be taught anything. Without any help from Mother or Father Robin, he made his first flight. It was a short flight, just to the nearest branch. But what a flight it was!

Jenny watched. Mother and Father Robin watched. His brothers and sister, who had just learned to leave the nest, watched. They could hardly believe their eyes. For his days in the box had had a strange result. Instead of taking off at a slant, like an airplane, the way all other robins do, he flew straight up into the air, from the ground straight up to the nearest branch. And then once again he took off straight into the air to the next branch. And to the next. How proud he was!

And no wonder there was such great astonishment among the birds. The catbird passed the word along to the other birds. The woodpecker stopped his rat-tat-tat on the tree to come and look; the brown thrush came, singing his friendly song. The handsome blue jay wanted to see too, and so did the little sparrows and wrens. They all wanted to see the youngest robin fly. For he was a celebrity. The robin who could fly straight up into the air! A helicopter bird! A whirly bird!